THE INTERLUDE

THE GALILEO PRESS LTD

Baltimore, Maryland

THE

INTERLUDE

Fables of the Twice-Fallen Angels

D.W. Fenza

Copyright © 1989 by D.W. Fenza

Published by The Galileo Press, Ltd., 15201 Wheeler Lane,
Sparks, Maryland 21152

Cover photograph: Christmas Kennedy Airport. 1967. Joel Meyerowitz. Gelatin-silver print, 9 × 13½". Collection, The Museum of Modern Art, New York. Purchase. Copy Print © 1989 The Museum of Modern Art, New York.

Design: Charles Casey Martin

Publication of this book was made possible in part by a grant from the Maryland State Arts Council

LIBRARY OF CONGRESS CATALOGING-IN-PUBLICATION DATA

Fenza, D. W. (David W.), 1955–
    The interlude : fables of the twice-fallen angels / by D.W. Fenza.
    — 1st ed.
        p.   cm.
    ISBN 0-913123-22-6 : $9.95 (est.)
    I. Title.
    PS3556.E58158   1989
    811'.54—dc19   89-1542
                                                        CIP

FIRST EDITION

"Can it be that any man has skill to fabricate himself?"
—*St. Augustine*

". . . They trespass, authors to themselves in all . . ."
—*Milton*

". . . the Mind is to herself
Witness and judge . . ."
—*Wordsworth*

0.

An archangel was marching before us—brandishing
a broken sword. We followed him through dunes,
over parched weeds, dry bones, and across the searing
vacancies. We pitched our tents below a single,
unblinking eye, which hovered above a pyramid. That gaze,
our goal, even the contents of our caravan—all
remained a mystery. We could only pose with wild hair,
sandblasted clothing, and our own vatic stares. Style
became our means and our end, which leaves the archangel
flashing his broken sword with the finesse
of a drum majorette. Now it's half-time
all the time.

1.

The hero of our tale, a lawyer whom we shall leave
unnamed—he stared beyond his balcony windows.
Over the city, the moon shone like a devalued coin.
The month of April, for him, was a cruel burlesque,
expensive, with heavy taxes. From the antique
loveseat where he sat, across the Oriental carpet to
the leather sofa where his wife sprawled, indifference
enclosed the room—a purse of frost. Meanwhile,
in the bosom of the desert, after the rocking
of our camels, after the wind pelted us with
scarves and boas of sand, after lewd glances from

that eye above the pyramid, after an excess of
unflattering light, I went walking alone. I found
the angel drawing in the sand with his broken sword.
In the moonlight and my sleeplessness, his face appeared
mercurial. Sometimes he resembled my father, sometimes
a woman I once knew, sometimes myself when I was younger.
We decided to improvise a tale to pass the night.
I would invent one chapter, then he the next, then I,
and so on, until we slept and our dreams interjected
parenthetical sequels—blossoms within blossoms.
At dawn, nodding on our camels again, we resumed
our tale. Our throats and voices withered in the heat,
but others would finish our episodes for us. Sometimes,
our caravan disagreed about the outcome of a scene.
From atop the backs of our camels, we shouted, flailing
our arms—each of us, a prophet with his own vision,
straddling his own mountaintop. I despaired that
there was no hope for our tale—there were
too many of them. Meanwhile, the lawyer descended
from his lofty condo to drink at his local bar;
and the angel climbed down from his camel to diagram
the plot of our story. Among rising and forking lines
of conflict, odd intersections like that between limbs
of flesh and wood, sad arrows like nails driven between
love in heaven and love here in the dirt, we knew
something, somewhere, had to be sacrificed.
On the streets where the lawyer went walking, the wind
lifted a page of newsprint and impaled it
on the branch of a sooty and budding tree.

1.414213 . . .

"Multiply and be fruitful," the sun-god said;
and below the linden trees, in lime-rich soil,
in darkness, the spores divided and grew;
and the Pythagoreans, for whom whole numbers
were divine, became troubled by the square root

of two, by all fractions sinking bottomless wells
into a netherworld of sunless fructifying,
irrational mates, endless divorces. Luckily,
the angels snorted like pigs and bloodhounds,
clawing the earth, until they exposed
truffles, the fruits of darkness.

2.

He wanted a systematic critique of the world
to complement his new appliances, but she
brought home a cynical colleague who
drop-kicked an entire tray of hors d'oeuvres.
She could only laugh as they all began
cleaning up the mess. In Holy John's day,
earth was only one remove from heaven,
and you could win admission through certain
humble contortions of self, without which
you would plummet, twice-removed, into hell.
On his hands and knees, picking up escargots,
which, earlier, he had stuffed into mushroom caps,
he felt ridiculous. Today, the contortions
seem mainly erotic, and heaven only imaginary;
and to be fallen from a place which is only
the dream of a place—*that*, godless ones, is to be
twice-fallen. The two of them made jokes
he failed to understand. She was bored, he knew,
with their household, and so they had mounted
the archetypal merry-go-round of loss and gain
again. He felt angry, absurd—an adult
still riding a painted pony.

3.

His old friends were all having children
and trading in their sports cars for more
practical sedans. Although the angels once rode

with the convertible roof down—their hair
whipping promiscuously about, and the noise
of their words passing behind them
as quickly as they were said—they now
duplicated and filed away their letters;
their hair was in place; they piloted their desks
as they would planes with no thrust, no wings.
Earlier in his marriage, when emptiness
was what he felt, his wife would play
snappy baroque tunes, which lightened his mood,
but now when he brought home his gloom,
her light airs were revolting, her gaiety
an offensive show of independence.

3.141592 . . .

Reckless driving may make you feel closer
to desire's mythical finish, but Archimedes
preferred drawing in sand since that medium
allowed quick revision. My twice-fallen
patron saint, Archimedes is perched upon
the rattling dashboard of my narrative.
To designate 1,000,000, the ancient Egyptians
drew the stick figure of a man with arms stretched
upwards in awe—or maybe it was a god embracing
the universe; but Archimedes decided
a million was neither large nor small enough
to be wondrous or godlike. He invented
a system of exponential notation
and integral calculus, by which he reached
a closer approximation of *pi*
and sums with more than 206,500 digits!
In the seventeenth century, a blind prophet
showed the soldiers of hell would play flutes
to charm their steps over the smoldering
lots of asphalt; so even far below, music
raises its shrubs of breath, its unreal
horticulture; the infernal also made

gold highways and a gold metropolis;
and Archimedes prefigured this vision
long before the blind prophet had been born:
in hell, we toil for the approximation
of ideals, not the blue ideals themselves;
in hell, there's no sensual deprivation,
only sorrow's exponential increase
for each garden, highway, and shopping mall
desire passes by, following
an endless map.

4.

She often babysat their friends' children,
who spilled soda on the Oriental carpet,
who molested the piano, who endangered
every vase and figurine in the house,
who made the stereo's tone arm jump
and rip through an entire fugue in the time
it takes two brats to jump off the sofa,
which had become a deep space cruiser
trashed by Z-rays from planet Phobos.
The imaginative launchings of children
are a form of discontinuity which frees them
from the stillness of museums, which was
the form of continuity he preferred.
The universe is 99% hydrogen and helium,
but he disdained simple building blocks
because, childless, he had never anticipated
the genesis—between bubbles of saliva—
of his child's first word.

5.

Tired of chasing game all day, the lion yawns
and watches the cubs stalk each other and pounce,
not yet knowing the fatal import of their practice.

Their games remind him of his long day, and he
would rather forget. He retires to his rock.
That was the trouble: he became more kingly
in his middle years and took fewer and fewer
angels seriously, until the angels knew it was
pointless to make their appeals. Because he found
work at the office so unpleasant, he expected
his home to be pleasure's ideal; so he dismissed
homely upsets with a roar, the sweep of his paw.
He desired stillness, silence, unchanging peace;
and he made them his kingdom's law.

6.

Sometimes we wish to be a restful tree
that holds an owl's knowing stare, its mantra
of one syllable naming the darkness.
When Odysseus had been especially
heroic, Athena blessed him with sleep
without dreams. I would never consider
dreamless sleep to be a gift, merely
a long, dead canal. Scientists tell us
that dreaming is necessary for rest,
that under closed lids the eyes must spin
this way and that, observatories focusing
on heavens of their own mad invention.
To be the hero of a goddess — that
is to be a walking dream, a figure
rippling with metaphor and muscles,
when each step, each act, advances the will
of the divine itinerary. Left behind
in our homely homes, we know history
as a complex of cluttered apartments
in which the rooms are a disheartening mess,
not because we hold too much, but because
our lifetimes are so small; so dreamlessness,
heavenly silence, the still point — all maintain

their specious appeal, launching a space race
to the barren moon of an absolute ideal.

7.

He told his clients and colleagues as little
about himself as was possible, for he had learned
the more you tell them, the more they suspect
you're too distracted to do the job; so
he became Nobody, just the man for the job.
To free himself and his men from the cave
of the Cyclops, Odysseus claimed to be Nobody;
but unlike Odysseus, the lawyer of our story
kept returning to the same cave, the same corporate
giants. He hardened his heart, sharpening
his pencils and wits, but he often missed
his mark, and felt he was being stared down
by a single, bloodshot, and unblinking eye.
He became so proficient at omitting
his life from work, he truly lost himself;
and for so great a sacrifice, he bound
his wife to an unspoken, unwritten
testament, obligating her to be his
heavenly reward, his dream, his rest. She
broke this contract, never knowing she'd been so
underwritten. Had she known, she would have
loudly refused to become the booty
of his sleep, a cloud-like fleece for his bed.
He felt betrayed nonetheless and dreamt
greater rewards (his prow nodding into
misty lagoons, a tan beauty running
her hands through his beard, tasting his salty
lips with hers, and so on . . .) until before him
his wife appeared—a pale traitor. She tried
to find in him the shy student—half-boy
half-man—with whom she had fallen in love

ten years ago. She saw the man was gone;
the boy, dead; and in their place,
Nobody . . .

8.

Anarchy has finally entered the world
of fashion; next year's dresses will be longer
and shorter while pants will be baggier
and tighter. Truths are variable also, and
the *artistes* discuss how noble it is *not*
to embrace any central truth. Unfortunately,
we must act, and most acts spring from an assumption
about the truth; and so positing truths in art,
even conflicting ones, is probably more useful
so we consumers can find the motivating,
twice-fallen angel we need. Even provisional ideas
hover angelically. Some angels hide
their wings in the shadows they cast, as they
want to appear less free for your sake, but when
you discover their wings, it's as though knives
were unsheathed. The marriage vandalizes itself;
your heart deflates with a serpentine hiss; and you
chainsmoke in a room where the sunlight has beaten
unmercifully on a painting for so long that its
apples and flowers have begun to fade.

9.

The more they dined on the fruit of knowledge,
the more unforgivable flaws they found
in the bread and wine of communion.
There were always more heavenly breads,
vintages of more grace and harmony—
an ideal union beyond this communion.
Preparing his banquet, he stripped each layer

of onion from the onion, only to bare
a green and bitter core. Self-pity, cooking,
and adultery are three of the great
indoor sports; and with some training, one may
engage in all three at the same time.
Each fearing that the other would soon serve
more masterful strokes, he and his wife practiced
their sweaty volleys. If variety is a spice,
promiscuity is life's intoxicating herb.
With too many chefs in a steamy kitchen—
an inferno of flambé and sauté—
they tried new recipes with salacious
vigor. They perfected a house specialty,
which emptied the house—two hearts
on a skewer, love's brochette.

10.

I am still fascinated by the geometrical notion
that, between two points, two other points may make
their points, and so on. This divisibility relates
to a new track of transcendental thought, but how
escapes me since, through the clatter of hooves,
the flutter of wings, I don't know who among my
many selves is speaking. The couple of our story
has harnessed a small chariot to an unruly herd
of horses with flaring nostrils and awesome legs;
surely the outstretched legs and flaming manes
are gestures of desire as they so quickly race
to become the ghosts of themselves. When desire sweeps
the triple crown of memory, imagination, and reason,
it may be better to relinquish the winner's cup
and find a way to make less more. Dividing and
multiplying a single subject is one way; and,
I believe, Archimedes knew this. Later we will have
much more to say about Archimedes, a prophet's
prophet, who stands as one of the first, great

modern poets. Suffice to say for now: he calculated
that love was simply the ratio of earth under heaven
times the self squared; but he soon saw this formula
was unworkable, except in demonstrating that love's sum
was more minutely subtle, more gorgeously vast
than he could reckon.

11.

The lawyer's arrogance was monumental, but just on
the periphery of his vision, small flashes
of guilt would bother some remote part
of his summer skies; lightning would stagger
just over the horizon, and he would notice
a friendly face freeze into a mask that hid
disgust at his proud displays; so he invented
trials of sorrow, or he exaggerated the sorrows
that were true to him, and he held each sorrow up
the way a Victorian lady might have held up
her parasol: to make her soul seem pale, so fair,
and too fine for the blatant light. In those
testimonies, he always portrayed himself
as the victim: the world shook him and rode him,
so hard, and he was the horse wincing in his stall
as the heavens flashed and blundered, as angels stumbled
and fell in heaps over the fields, the trees, the rooftops;
but some tales betray their own teller,
and his own airs undid him. A door slammed,
not shut, but open, as love departed; and he felt
the draft as the spirit of his home followed her,
as his lies, his shadows, coupled vainly within all
the emptiness of his house. He realized that
to make the fables come true, he must become
their victim; so that, for example, her departure
would have a greater effect than even she had planned.
Drunk, treading his reflection on the wet,
city streets, he began planning the decorous disregard

he would show for his life; but after a month or so
of his performances, he could no longer tell
the actor from his true self, and he was vaguely sad
to find that he no longer wanted her back,
nor did he want himself back; he merely wanted
to walk into the storm without his umbrella,
to be extinguished, gone, along with the city's sour haze
that the cold rain will drive back into the ground.

12.

The twice-fallen angels had torn their epaulets
from their shoulders, their medals from their chests,
the gold bars of their ranks from their sleeves.
They broke their sabers over their knees, and then went
to insult the king with their independence,
their resignation; but they found an empty crown
on an empty throne. They found their lawbooks
were burning; their spouses, missing.
Useless and colorful as autumnal leaves, useless
and colorful as the dollar bills of a failed confederacy,
the epaulets and insignias fell behind them
as they flew, unbearably light, into the twilight.

13.

He represented a company, which operated factories in
a dozen states, but which dumped its waste in all fifty;
rather than really do something about the problem,
the company spent millions on advertising to
dramatize a patriotic concern. The gulf between
impressive fronts and real solutions gives itself,
eagerly, to anyone willing to destroy a fine career.
The invention of Christ marked a shift in emphasis
to the suffering of the individual, away from
the suffering of the tribe, the gloomy exodus

of families leaving in stormy, patriarchal review.
Sometimes he feared that his self had been
reduced to an air conditioner humming stupidly
between a pleasant climate and a nasty one.
With his law firm and home humming along,
he allowed a real crisis to blossom, so he could
sweat like hell all summer. A romantic storyteller
would blame his passion, but his analyst indicated
a center of self-hate as the real mover and shaker.
The twice-fallen angel recognized it as the impulse
towards martyrdom, common as any city intersection
and just as flashy with sirens, billboards, and lights.
One effaces one's self at the office, which makes one
tend to self-indulge, later, to compensate; and perhaps,
this is the worst from the two worlds of tribe and self.
The mind stores cassettes which replay our best,
most proven songs of generosity, and of sorrow;
and unwinding at the bar, he played his greatest hits;
but neither the blond nor her tan friend were impressed,
since the plain facts demonstrated his loneliness,
which left him without any true center. On the freeway,
a hubcap will occasionally spring loose from its wheel
and go skittering across the pavement, the way an obsolete
self-image ditches itself. The next morning, he felt
as though he were lost in tall weeds among beer cans.

14.

Because none of the ideals are really fixed,
some angels have sagging breasts and have been seen
pushing shopping carts. Each page is the face
of an angel, on which you have declared love,
apologized, ridiculed world events, or closed
that big deal. Each word, a wound, a bruise.
The angels take their accusations and hurts
to the waiting rooms of truth, and everyone
refuses to pay the bill. A common fault

with young painters is that they promote
their own sensitivities before they show
the angels basking in an otherly light;
sometimes this light seems heartless because
it includes more souls than you can see
in a single thought. This light is visible
if you rise early enough, happy to remain within
the moment, each moment, but not if you're just
in a hurry to get through the fucking day.

15.

She had withdrawn from the alliance by slow degrees,
although, for what it was worth, the treaty remained.
He wakes up and his hands smell like his hands. Once,
at work, he smelled her scent on his hands, and gladly
he took on the piles of documents before him, a boy again
running through autumnal leaves just to be running
through autumnal leaves; but now his hands were just
his hands, work was work, tick-tock. She sold high-tech
medical scanners. Her work often took her abroad,
to France; and she sent him postcards, but fewer
as months passed. He imagined the time when she, sitting
in some cafe, would mention to a friend that, yeah,
she was married once, then pass on to other topics
without stopping to name him. It worried him that
his passage to namelessness might be less leisurely
than the sun's decline as it swaddles the plazas
in amber and rose, glinting off the wine glasses
at the cafe, where she decides what to do for dinner.
In a bar, he met a man who said he had been on the deck
of an aircraft carrier that was circling in the tropics
during a hydrogen bomb test. With his hands, he covered
his eyes against the blast; but he still saw the flash
through pale shadows, through the flesh, the bones of his hands.
When the bar closed, the ex-sailor left alone; he left alone;
starlight—small waves, big waves, x-rays,

and other rays, alpha to omega—a shower of lights
racing through and beyond us, as if we were a moment
not worth stopping for or recounting . . .

16.

Dear X, after a long siege of words at my desk,
I took a walk north, to our old neighborhood,
to extrapolate on the sun's decline on this
misty day. Of course, the facades on many
of the townhouses had changed, and I had
trouble identifying our old apartment.
What's difficult when you're alone is to walk
in the city, to walk beneath the gaze
of thousands of city windows, and to realize
no one is looking forward to your next move;
it's enough to make your next move spiteful,
or desperate.

17.

Adultery is, at first, convenient because
it supplies the whiteness of an unfinished
story, like the desert sands where the prophets
would cast their suggestive shadows. That blankness
promises everything to someone immolated,
half-alive, within a ridiculous job.
Repetition often appears more mechanical
than natural, therefore the antithesis of life
for the postmodern self who places
a premium on the unique, and who may feel
foolish dancing while sober, especially if
the D.J. is blasting the smash hit single
overplayed in hearts and cities everywhere.

18.

Because he was a good, Irish Catholic lad,
he drank heavily before his promiscuous supplications;
but when he became ill, the guilt lunged out
like a many-headed jack-in-the-box. The trinity
sprang from a divisive anxiety of self,
which the desert sun brought to a fabulous boil
long ago, when the towns were far less crowded
and the company was needed.

19.

Sometimes pleasure lays itself down like obsequious
pavements that keep the earth from rupturing into
the anarchy of weeds, thorns, and burrs; and then
your chest fills with the boring exhaustion of so many
pigeons slumbering among the charred rafters
of an abandoned barn. The rain and ashes,
as you recall a stranger unbuckling your belt.
Regret is the after-shade of mere eroticism,
the rain admonishing itself in the nearest puddle,
a numbing penumbra the moon wallows within —
a dark mirror, the cool lips of a shadow.

20.

Dear X, Last night, I got drunk for no purpose;
the fourth drink did not even make me daring,
which sometimes leads to a new friendship,
a strange apartment. I just drank towards sleep . . .

21.

At the office, he began imagining conversations
among the twice-fallen. Because pure thought
has no issue but death, it's important to dress

abstractions in flesh so they may mate and give
to the earthly cornucopia. His suit was wrinkled;
his lapel smelled of gin. He had no idea sorrow
held so many fragrant folds, embracing itself,
petal around petal, his prize-winning rose.
When taking the bar exam, there is a section
which asks, "Which answer is the least correct?"
A world which asks questions like that is enough
to make anyone sigh, shrug, and then claim
a seven-digit income, just for spite. His colleagues
were unamused by his newly regained sense of irony,
and they decided to replace him; but since all
the answers were correct, he refused to argue.
He emptied his desk. The fragrance of gin
and roses sustained him through lunch.

22.

Dear X, Unlike all the windows of the city,
the church windows seem to maintain
the illusion that they are watching you.
The wounds of all the martyrs are windows
addressed to you. You look in and see
the pain of virtue you shrugged off long ago.

23.

Angels are often called in to make the same old door
seem capable of dramatic new exits and starts.
How could we children stay indoors when we could
shout as so many heroes or victims outside? The door,
as we came and went, slammed behind us—an exclamation
our parents tolerated with our exuberance which made
their blood thrill in small ways at least. Older,
the same entrances and exits, pomp, and slams,
but the games demand more taxing performances

and violence. We believe we're just rehearsing when
the show folds forever—the door slams, and it locks.

24.

Dear X, I was having lunch at the harbor,
and sooty shrouds of snow were dissipating
in the thick fog of the afternoon when
a woman decided to walk down the pier, undress,
and drown herself. She left her clothing,
purse, and suicide note on the pier.
At rush hour, they were still dredging
for her body. Some of the police were
working overtime, which suited them fine.
No one could tell me her name.
The newspapers ignored the incident,
and I was hoping to read her note.
Perhaps she placed the blame on someone,
or on all the city's cold-hearted windows,
or on some pure thought that, like any cathedral,
fills with death even when flushed with light,
the glow of rose windows . . .

25.

A bus spewed a cloud of gray fumes; within
himself, he felt a corresponding exhaustion.
That burden of his own unnatural self
he carried, like a courier lugging around
a fat briefcase chained to his wrist. He'd love
never to work, but his work-a-day self
provides shelter, goods. Sure, he can kick ass—
take home a case file thick as a phone book,
and by morning, pose a serpentine snare,
the motions and appeals to tie up, to take in
the taxpayers' dollars and corporate cash.

He can charm the client, manipulate
the jury—easy as playing a jukebox.
He sought employment, tried to sell the self
that worked and whirred like a clean machine;
but he chortled, stalled; and beneath the hood,
they found his dolphin-smile, his mocking eyes.
Walking home, wishing he could still believe
goods were goodness, he saw a man sleeping
beneath a heap of trash. Employed or unemployed,
he felt the weight of many a weary day,
not his, and such as were not made for him.

26.

Dear X, Years ago, during summers between terms
of school, I would work as a roustabout.
At the mill, the bearings squealed; the air quivered
in waves of heat over the hot presses;
and we would dismount the half-ton roll
of paper from its spool, and push it towards
the waiting arms of the fork-lift. Dead-tired
by noon, I felt empty-headed, as if I had
a slight fever; my tongue felt thick with thirst,
with dust and sweat, the spices of mortality.
If our condition of twice-fallenness continues,
we will have more artists than patrons of the arts,
and art will degrade work. As for the revolution
that raised the workers, it has petrified
into large bureaucracies which prohibit
truly free revolts, among which art stands
as the most stylish angel; so mechanical labor
will retain its sameness and equality, making each
moment empty as the last, just like death,
the great equalizer, tossing the spices
of mortality in every lunchbox—
a little dust, a little salt.

27.

After some unpromising job interviews,
he took in a movie matinee for
the escapist oblivion one expects
from a motion picture with no conscience.
A Western set in Mexico: a stranger
rides into town, works as a gunslinger
for two opposing clans; the clans ravage
each other while he takes their women and gold;
the gunfighters who remain—he shows them
his revolver's fatal flash; and they fall
in ecstatic heaps of twisted torsos
and limbs. Throughout the movie, the stranger
is nameless, called only "the American"
by both clans. Watching a nameless hero
is annoying at first, but namelessness
partakes of the formlessness of death, dreams,
and mindless pleasure—the kisses and abysses
in which the twice-fallen lose themselves.
Besides, a name is static, but the self,
if heroic, is not. At an airport once,
he saw a supersonic airliner, nose-up,
roaring, taking off to leave even its
own noise behind itself. He desired that flight—
sublime, angelic, inhuman.

28.

One may forfeit heaven and hope, instead, to regain
paradise; and sometimes this exchange seems as easy
as jumping off a bridge or sleeping with your spouse's
best friend. Some dreams share the ambivalence
of light, asserting the properties of a mass without
actually being a mass. A dream, in the first few
moments of waking, may seem like a hazy bridge

at dawn. The piers, the arching cables, the girders
are barely discernible through the pale gauze
of moist air; yet the bridge is more interesting
for being obscure, arching through the limits of vision,
like the outcome of your supplication for an evening
of love, or for a merciful landing upon the cool,
mossy couches of paradise. More subversive than you
expected, the dream may become something else
as you try to remember it: thinking becomes thanking;
the victim is torn limb from limb, thrown
to the river and swept away, only to become the soil
of a tree through which he rises again, as a god.
But then, the dream may also die and stay dead
according to the sunlit laws of common sense. You drive
to the bridge, and it's just another public thoroughfare.
Or you continue to stare at the bridge from a distance
until it vanishes at noon because the busy air
becomes brighter than the bridge, just as each dawn
the atmosphere glares away the stars, except the one,
overbearing, at our orbit's dead center.

29.

Like God's foreknowledge of Original Sin,
the linoleum floors of the state office building
have that ugly, dappled pattern in which
scuffs and cigarette burns appear as part
of the design. He once thought a sandwich
with too much mayonnaise best symbolized
the malaise of our aesthetic consciousness,
but he had not yet seen the fog lingering for hours
outside the administration for the unemployed.

30.

Basking themselves in that eternal light,
the angels recline in beach chairs before

the vast commotion of humanity, its history,
its prospects. At first the sea amuses them
as they watch some mortals rise above others,
fail, and then turn white in the ebullience
of their downward rush. The urgency,
the mortal blood the moon makes race, the angels
cannot understand since each wave, each soul,
embraces only itself and, in its conclusion,
the shifty beach. The angels decide that either
everything matters or nothing does. The angels
yawn, roll over, and begin tanning their backs,
cooled by the undulations of their wings.

31.

From shock to shock, from new test to
lost contest—that's no way to raise a family,
but it's a way of becoming an archangel
in the trashed casinos of desire. During holidays,
he usually felt compelled to sulk, although
formal obligations are what make skin-tight clothing
so interesting. The archangel, for a souvenir,
keeps the broken sword of his self-demotion,
and he smiles like one about to transgress
the polite limits of a dinner date.

32.

To celebrate his downward mobility, he
and an athletic stranger engaged in
fashion's vivisection, with clothing strewn
all over the apartment—useless remnants.
Their experiment was a success as their nakedness
concealed their souls with the usual subterfuge
of tenderness. He was happy like a sailor
brought to his knees upon the heaving deck—

the rope sliding through his burning hands—
the mast buckling. Self-imposed loss springs from
our modern leisures, which afford so many
choices that, of course, we must choose one hand
while taking the elegy of the other. Because love
had left on a jet plane last year, the kisses
remain like trampled violets in a garden;
and his tall ship the stranger merely sank,
and he was only glad to have drunk so deeply.
Sometimes we look back on the younger man who launched
this passion or that ambition, and we can't understand
that admiral's motives, although they were our own.
There have been too many sunken ships, too many seas
that have looked the same, and our identity rises,
a yellow sail with monstrous stitching crossing itself
in memory of the slashing winds and the cries
of those swept away. The remembered only become holy
when we live in the same neighborhood a long time,
so that the landscapes and people we encounter
are also remembered people and places, and each face
recalls its memory; and then the mind can rest its thoughts,
so buoyantly, upon the world that made them.

33.

Because Frankenstein's creature was born
an adult, learning in a year what it takes us
an entire childhood and adolescence to learn,
he went mad, of course, with no innocence
to let ideals ripen, or to darken, bronze,
like sunbathers on the beach. With no heaven
to place the angels of guilt and mercy
in his heart, his thoughts were blunt stones,
monuments to worldwide justice: victims
victimizing those responsible for their scars.
Remember the old beaches? The parks? When you,
not recognizing the world's cruelty as law,

sometimes tried to behave better than yourself,
and sometimes, you even succeeded? But now,
clouds rage, the sky breaks, and mountainous,
you wake to find yourself, the monster
of your own bed.

34.

Murder is merely a craft; suicide,
an art. Murder repeats the banality
of evil for pragmatic ends: fixing a muzzle
on dissent, expediting an inheritance, control
of the drug trade in the West End, and so on.
Suicide, on the other hand, partakes
of art's high uselessness, relinquishing
power, except an infinitesimally small force
acquired through altering the symbols of things
but not the things themselves. His death,
he thought, would be prophetic, prefiguring
the world's closing statement of windfall
victims and earnings. At first, his self-hate
coupled with arrogance—his assumption
that he could be so vastly meaningful;
but then he had his doubts; so he sentenced himself
to writing sentences, a long suicide note
to augment his fall.

35.

Dear X, It's no accident that suffering has its place,
fixed with nails, in the New Testament. There's
nothing like pain to make you want to leap away
from your flesh, while, like festive lights
on a tree at night, the corporeal limits glow.
The self feels the world, but suspended there,
dreams another. Bored with both riverbanks, lovers

may perch midway on the highest arc of a bridge
for a precarious view. Suspension of self happens
before tenses fall into the order of monuments;
so if young lovers speak too drunkenly or too
somberly, you know they have parked on that bridge.

36.

The news reported that six miles of ice
had broken away from Antarctica,
turning the ocean into a marvelous
cocktail. He imagined whole ecosystems
thrown into shock as it shivered away
towards tropical coasts. He envied it, too,
the speculation it aroused about
global temperatures, our world growing
hellish, with rising tides. If only he
could engender such concern, his demise
would be the stroke of legends and hearts
everywhere! It would only hurt for a while,
then dissolve like a hangover into
a fresh drink. He had decided to jump
from a bridge—that would hurt and therefore
be manly, and the tide would take him to
a vacancy, remarkable and lunar.
First, depravity breaks out like a winning
smile, then spreads, zipperless and cancerous;
none the less, God says it can be dissolved
by water, many dark days and deeper nights
of water, letting the few couples still afloat
restore the good. None of his father's friends
did themselves in; they all worked, retired,
and died in their small homes. His father's pal,
next door, was overly wide and chesty with
a triple-by-pass inside; he barbecued until
October. When warned about steaks and beer,

he shrugged with his brilliant non sequitur,
"The kids are all married now. I did good."
He had, and he died. Our nameless hero
knew he was refining a talent (latent
in everyone) for final things, but not
for the first. From upon high, his childless
condominium, he bore his broad smile,
no good—an ark of ice.

37.

When he took the Angel of Continuity
by the hand, he had no idea that
her senile father, Angel of Boredom,
would become their first dependent.
Filling out his tax forms, he began to wish
he were exempt from everything. His watch
measured all the moments he couldn't wait
to pass *through*, as if he could reach
an hour he would be glad to rest *within,*
when a lavish rain covers a parched garden,
a rose folding into itself to be itself.
Lumbering through the cycles of work and home,
he had gained self-knowledge, but at the expense
of becoming a predictable satellite,
which, he found, wasn't really worth knowing.
And so he came to kneel before the Angels
of Discontinuity, their cheeks flushed,
their windblown hair, as the exalting
blasts of the unplanned swept over them;
but he soon saw that the blueprints were only
the slashes of vandals, that the building
was askew, and that the dangerous scaffolds
had become the permanent hallways and stairs.
Before the window, through open slats
of the venetian blind, he watched the moon

as it rose, one slat at a time, as if
it had been climbing a ladder. Since the moon had
no heaven, only the sky, that climbing,
he shrugged, was only another chore.

38.

Over his breast or back upon his haunch,
his wallet rode like another organ,
one he had gained with manhood—artificial,
but vital nonetheless. You need money
in mega-heaps, to hold nature close;
otherwise, you can afford only cheap
formica tables, a veneer bookcase,
vinyl upholstery, polyester suits,
drinks and food with bogus ingredients,
and trips to the shore—a receding beach
so trussed by hotels, condos, shops, and cars
that the folding surf is all that remains
of the Great, Green Mother, her breathy lullaby.
His wallet, he knew, was the nexus, the synapse
between him and long stays in the mountains,
between him and deep repose in a pastoral lap,
between him and the next drink, between him
and a sublime dinner date. The mattress
of promiscuity is stuffed with cash to make
the bed more posh; but in the metropolis,
amid the steel, glass, asphalt, concrete, and brick,
the expense seems worth it since that bed gives
swift access to nature's soothing valleys and rills.
The credit card companies, however, cancelled
his membership. Unemployed, his savings spent,
he shrank to a feeble, self-conscious nub.
Following the low tide of dollars and cents,
the Green Mother and her nymphs withdrew,
glancing back over bare shoulders, laughing
at his wallet's detumescence.

39.

The rain mixes with smog and then corrodes
stone buildings and monuments. The statues
have wept long, sooty streams. Watching the rain,
the shimmering streets and trees, he drank brandy
and ate cookies till he was sleepy and numb.
He tossed his wife's unanswered letters
to the unruly heap on the table.
His wallet had grown empty, slim; but he had grown
fat. No one thing satisfied him; so he
devoured many, hoping their hefty sum
would cancel his discontent. Wet leaves
are a disguise; the red and yellow leaves,
just a more brilliant subterfuge. The soul
of a tree is its pith, the core at which
the concentric rings stop. The innocent
will say: A sapling soon grows those layers
so that it can embrace more earth, more sky;
the experienced will say: The soul grows
sheathing around sheathing because it needs
insulation. Wider, he was warmer, too,
tucking himself in to dream and admire
the still resolve of trees. Let the impure rain
spatter across his boughs; upon his bark,
let lovers carve their tentative hearts.
Far within, his soul circled to contain
itself, true and untouched.

40.

After the Angels of Realty threatened foreclosure
on his decadent garden, he went walking in the city,
which gathers sorrow as gutters take the rain.
If you say hello to strangers on the street,
you cultivate feelings of threat, ridicule,
resentment, indifference, and so on. The human order,

you see, is too fractious. There's an order
bigger than earth's pastoral law, more grand
than the merry-go-round of seasons leaving
and coming again. There's the order of
atoms, planets, stars, galaxies, and all
the emptiness and subtle forces among them.
The Being of all things, whose umbrella we solicit,
is a lover whose form we may never recognize;
so, deeply obscure, in the shade with a shade,
we enjoy a little shelter, although the umbrella's
shaft, ribs, and sheathing seem to have been made
from extinct animals; and in store windows,
spotted and veined with falling water, we see
our reflections darkly.

41.

Many of the successful rehabilitation programs
advance from the assumption that life is worth
staying straight and sober for, and a very
business-like God is usually behind all this,
ready to co-sign a new loan on your good intentions
and clear-headedness; but after staying sober
for what seemed eternity, he esteemed his life
even less than before. Although his handwriting
had become more legible, what he had to say
was more unbearable. His counselors reminded him
about his goals, how important it was to
"*image*" them, to be organized around those
images; and so he raised a few icons of
commerce and intimacy to his heart; the dazzle
of spiritual renewal he made coincide with
the glimmer of freshly minted coins, with
sequins on a dress, with chrome hood ornaments
on long limousines—the flash of glamour.
Like an arcade, his heart shimmered and rang;
and he found this arcade was no place
where he could live.

42.

The trouble with prophecies is that soon,
like boats and blossoms, they become obsolete.
One Chinese poet folded his poems
into boats, tucking this pride into that
illusion, making himself small again,
sealing the written page within creases
of its blank reverse; and he gave those boats
to the river. He recalled a lost love,
the gleam of sweat on her back; and he wrote
about dew on a garden's marble stairs.
Half-sober priest, and half-drunken lover,
he wades knee-deep in water. Love improves
on the glittering rift between this world
and the void, where it can't be exchanged
for mere pleasure or pay. It drifts away.
The small paper boat takes in the river,
and the river takes it in.

43.

He no longer lived in his lofty condo.
He and his wife had rented their old home
so that, with the new income, they could pay
his mounting debts till he found work. Monthly,
she mailed him a check; he liked that—the money
came to him, rather than he seeking it.
It's good to be the king—when the world,
if she desires your attention, must come
to you. One king was so impressed with his
hefty serving of beef that he knighted it;
but as rush hour began, our leading man
drank cheap gin for dinner, blinking
and blanking out on a wobbly kitchen chair.
As if he were wearing a heavy crown,
his head drooped; then he slept atop his own
groaning table. And the world?—oh, she came
and went, while he slouched, sadly unable.

44.

"Bottoming out" he found himself merely
a character in his own twisted fable.
At his rehabilitation program, everyone
had a story to tell: those moments when
the tellers saw that the stories of their lives
had fallen to bizarre extremes, and that they,
the tellers, had to disassociate themselves
from their own badly written plots. He saw
he wore his despair like a water-drenched
overcoat, that his melodrama had grown
unfit to show his true self, although
he had conceived it, fall by fall, drop
by drop, until the flood began to mount
the walls of his house.

45.

He rented a one-bedroom apartment
on the ground floor of a row house. His new
neighborhood consisted of warehouses,
loading docks, bars, diners, more row houses,
and a bakery. In bed at night, he heard
the squealing and hissing of trucks as they
picked up the soft cargo of yeasty loaves.
He woke to the smell of warm bread. Again,
he considered jumping off a bridge, but
went out to buy gin instead. He stopped at
a shop of curios and junk and found
a stained and yellowing score of two-part
inventions, like those his wife had once played.
Although he didn't play himself, he bought
the score, and carried it home with his gin.
He cried and drank. He wrote an illegible
letter to his wife, closing it with "*thanking
of you.*" By noon, he had toppled onto

the floor. Staring at the balls of dust,
smelling bread and hearing the trucks pass by,
he heard it faintly begin—even there
among the crying wheels of commerce—
the unlikely duet of thinking
and thanking.

46.

You shouldn't hide from your own confessions
because soon you'll be taking the quirks of your past
and imposing them as laws on the rest of us;
but you can't interview yourself with the stereo playing
so loudly, and notice how the music remains, finally,
beyond words, allowing a certain promiscuity of thought,
which suits you fine since, in the tumult, you can forget
your cruelty. The notion of transcendence presupposes
ethical, aesthetic, and psychological hierarchies.
"The couple separated due to irreconcilable notions
of transcendence." At the crossroads of what you did
and what you should have done, the angel of guilt
is gossiping with your parents, in-laws, ex-lovers,
ex-employers, and estranged spouse; and in memory of this
intersection, you draw an enormous *X* across your face
in the mirror. You sing loudly at first, befriending
the entire orchestra; but your accompaniment fails
because you walk like a fucking animal, you forget
birthdays, shrugged away colleagues, and wasted
ten years of her life; and all too soon, the final
movement closes with your melody reduced to the
wheezing of one plaintive, and fading, violin.

47.

Dear X, I know that the mind is a nervous tree,
and spirits animal and philosophical roost there,
bending the branches, low. Sometimes, conversation

is the natural catapult of these spirits, and
the branches swing back up with a cheery rush.
The trouble is: sometimes aesthetic playfulness
is more attractive and liberating than ethics
which hang ropes from trees and hammer nails
in such unfriendly positions. I have heard
the evidence against me.

48.

He often imagined kissing her in the rain,
in one of those romantic triumphs over adversity.
Reclining with his back to the earth, he stares into
the sky as it plummets into itself; he decides
the sky is his pieta, a woman in a blue robe
swaddling the dark space of her unborn child,
the emptiness blessed with freedom. Having denied
everything, he found himself free to try on
various philosophies, as though he were a boy
trying on the hats of dead fathers. Now,
when love calls, from the other side of the world,
it's her noon to his sunset, her dawn to his midnight;
maybe it was a dictum of reversals that drove them
so far apart, so they could walk in a blasted orchard
where all the trees are up-ended, roots splaying
to the blue and white heavens. So many delusions
marketed themselves as successful screenplays,
calling for a madonna in evening dress, a father
in dark blue suit with matching fedora; but the roles
had failed to move him; and he remained his own
only child. He never kissed her in the rain;
and now as before, more than a body of water
held itself between them.

49.

Dear X, The clean shirts rising and falling
in the laundromat dryers are twice-fallen angels

ensnared by a maelstrom of passion and practicality.
I do not put all that much faith in intuition
since sometimes, like a reckless child, it arranges
all of its toys, pell-mell in the dark, for you
to trip over. Over the years, I've developed
a palate for wine, ethnic foods, and fine cigars;
and friends associate me with these attributes,
and I encourage them since they prove easy
starting points for conversation — unlike
the bizarre tribunal of selfhood, which keeps
overturning its own sentences in a whirl of heat
and lawlessness; besides, when travelling about
in France, it's still meaningful to inquire
what chateau or what neighborhood makes a certain
product, rather than what faceless corporation.
I put on my shirt, still warm from the dryer;
and turning up the collar, I thought I felt
your breath at my ear.

50.

Stranded on an island with his arch enemy,
a withered angel was trying to choose between
justice with a vengeance and justice with mercy.
A pagan, he favored a fatal vengeance, but that
would finish his fable abruptly, and someone
must preserve his story after death slams the door
to his room; and without his enemy, he might
deprive himself of someone else to tell the legend
of his ruddy dreams, of the lurid upheavals, devious
taproots, and generous blossoms.

51.

Your first step of transcendence is loss, and this loss
includes your idea of transcendence. From the ocean floor
to the mountains' apex, you chart your course;
but along the way, you fall in love with a voluptuous

valley. Meanwhile, the mountains still wear their icy masks
and share windy circumlocutions with the sea—too cold,
too dark, in their intimacy; so you choose to remain
between, between. He wanted to be held, nursed, but then
he felt too great for any pitiful subordination.
He tore his confessions in two—in a rift between
seducing the world and rebuking it. He littered his room
with crumpled balls of paper the size of angry fists
and disengaged hearts. When hypocrisy creates
a fault line, then it's likely the ground there
will quake with laughter. His monument and its lawn
began shaking. He worried that he might accidentally
be hit by a car and killed, before he had a chance
to finish his suicide note.

52.

It was a real estate agent's dream: the volcano
erupted and the lava flow added hundreds of new acres
to the island. The trees, however, were greatly
simplified: each survivor holding only one or two
leafless limbs; each standing alone, so far from others
in the vacant fields of pumice and ash. The old angel
took his arch enemy there, where everything appears
in shades of gray. In glaring opposition, the red fountain
that had risen over the crater was an accusing finger,
rising out of a wound; it was the angel's nightmare:
it was of the earth, yet wasted the earth.
They walked to where the forest resumed, and then sat
within a patch of red anthurium. With their friends
now flourishing on distant islands, and with others
now drifting, lost forever, to the ozone or the sea,
they found each other more tolerable, sitting among
the clownishly phallic and heartshaped flowers—
the long, yellow filaments drooping from red blossoms.
He laughs and hears its echo in his ex-rival's laugh.
From beneath a singed wing, the angel produces a flask

of wine, and they begin drinking into the twilight,
talking, and each plucking, for the other,
the inflamed and exotic flowers.

53.

Dear X, The Angel of Instant Gratification
and the Angel of Deferred Contentment
draw, unfortunately, from the same account—
yours. It's difficult to balance the figures
when the Angel of Instant Gratification leaves you
with countless overdrafts. Suicide is an escape
from these angels, their abysmal deficit, although
you never know when the Angel of Deferred Contentment
is going to place a fantastic blossom beneath your head,
so that what you dream assumes a natural course,
so that what you desire and what you accomplish seem,
for the moment, to be a beautiful lover swimming above
a beautiful reflection.

54.

The winter air has certain springtime pretensions,
which, later, will develop into a mature art, breaking
the sullen, cold meditations and pathetic bare limbs
with silly green off-shoots, while an animal slyness
will seem to lubricate all your joints, as you walk
and have sex differently in the uncommon air.
A prima ballerina lifts her right foot as high
as her right ear, and he takes this to be a gesture
of salacious pleasure, while she means it to be a
display of self-mastery. How many times you've misread
love's figure to be all ideals; and this, of course,
was more than love could bear, and you were calling
the overwrought air to your breast, and all you held was
the moon whittled away by the edge of a darkening dream.

The imagination has its sad inertia, too; but sometimes,
once you begin relating everything in sympathy,
its figurative embrace, it's not long before
sympathy seems greater than you although it's only
an aspect of you. While deliberating on his long
suicide note, he saw that his harshest sentences
had been overturned by more liberal successors;
and he was amazed at how much a sentence
could include, a train spouting its tumultuous
script of smoke, climbing the trestles of a bridge,
hauling such diverse travellers and freight;
and he was no longer sure which stop
would be his; and there, smoldering across
dark water, he felt relieved, and overruled.

55.

Dear X, Nothing is as self-immolating as the belief
that childhood is over. Brick after brick,
you have built an alley with no outlet,
and the city begins business as usual with
someone else at your desk. Madness, however,
is a splendid workshop, except for the red blossoms
of the wounded bringing the tools down
upon themselves; but like adolescence, nothing
is complete while everything is suggested.
A school bus full of younger selves shout and laugh,
and I have no idea where they are going.

56.

You be mortise to my tenon, and we will be
fixed for life, but too static, like a chest
of drawers filled with the shabby fashions
of an obsolete era; so never say to true love
"Please stay", because that is like asking love

to kiss Death's hand on its horny knuckles.
Once consciousness dies it no longer changes,
although it's subject to gossip by souls
surviving you, which gives your biographer
plenty to consider while your friends enjoy
at least one evening of really extreme
drinking and hobnobbing to consecrate your absence
with skull-smacking hangovers the next day.
Because paradise is lost and we must do something
with its perishable fruits, we must employ a comic
distance, so the self may step aside from itself
and then push itself in the direction of that
banana peel—a hip-wrenching fall on the waste
of paradise, which, Freud would say, is like knocking
your dentures off the nightstand while having
a nightmare of impotence. Last night, I had a dream
that I was driving a schoolbus; and when
the road forked, I had no idea which way
to go. Just outside my hometown, a schoolbus
crashed through guardrails and somersaulted down
a steep embankment. Surely the sorrow of young ideas
sailing to their oblivion is no proper retribution
for their being young, or ideas. The sadness of
a fallen nest with broken, blue eggs—a sign of
Spring's lack of mercy.

57.

Dear X, One shoe hits the floor, then the other. A sign
presents its wilted blossom. Your mate comes to bed
in silence. Is it the silence of fatigue? Resignation?
Resentment? Boredom? Indifference? Or just relief?
Perhaps it's a non-vintage blend of many harvests,
both sweet and blighted, of both the sadly withdrawn
and the promiscuously perfumed. You convince yourself
it's only a silence of fatigue, because, if it's not,
it demands inquiries, depositions, more inquiries,

further appeals, and so on; and you would rather sleep.
It's the chronic ambiguity of life that prepares one,
willy-nilly, to be a great reader of poems. In this case,
however, you are guilty of voluntary misreading
because you wanted the easy way out, the plush blankness
of your pillow; but later you have a dream that loses
video contact while the audible track remains: a heart
putters along, stalls, gives two resounding thumps,
then quits. You begin feeling anxious, sorry;
so you wake up to pose a question or a kiss, which is
the business of all well-adjusted poems; but the bed
is empty, and neither your mate's clothing nor shoes
remain behind because, for far too long, you insisted
on interpretations so simple they became an extension
of dreamless sleep; so love took its short lyric
of two shoe-thumps and a sigh
somewhere else for revision.

58.

An angel appeared before St. Theresa with a long,
golden dart, tipped with fire. Of this encounter
she said, "I thought he thrust it through my heart
several times, and that it reached my very entrails.
As he withdrew it, I thought it brought them with it,
and left me all burning with a great love of God.
So great was the pain that it made me give those moans;
and so utter the sweetness that this sharpest of pains
gave me, that there was no wanting it to stop, nor
is there any contenting of the soul less than God.
The pain is not physical, but spiritual." This passage
revels in the carnality it denies, just as carnal gestures
often seem to signify more than themselves. "Working
out," "Dining out," "Stepping out," "Burning out,"
we're all so anxious for our allotted ecstasy, even if
it's only drugs, athletic weariness, or salmon poached

in champagne with herbs, cream, and artichoke hearts.
An ex-lover underlined her favorite passages,
and rereading those sentences, my thoughts take
an undercurrent which seeks her. St. Theresa said,
"Prayer always means progress," voicing, I'm afraid,
a dissatisfaction with the moment's limits, which is
not unlike our nostalgia, or our impatience at rush hour.
Sometimes a kiss distracts one with the remembrance
of other kisses, which prohibits the seclusion
lovers desire. As Bernini sculpted St. Theresa's ecstasy,
her clothing is charged with countless folds and ripples
to suggest that this embrace comprised endless
smaller embraces. Another anti-theology yawns, the empty
foundation of a demolished building.

59.

Because he always admired the yellowing lace
on his grandmother's marble endtables,
the contrived handiwork upon the haphazard
whorl of stone, the lace embracing itself
and the emptiness that makes possible
the design of hearts and loops, because he
had stolen reams of legal pads from the office,
because poetry is as obscure as legalese,
he transformed his suicide note into
a long poem. He called it *The Intermission,*
for the goal of the poem was to offer
a truthful vision between revisions —
a garden's wingswept shade, its ripening
light, a hefty globe of fruit falling from
a knowledgeable tree — insufficient
in itself, but content to be fallen
having gathered a history of earth and sky
in its flesh, and bearing, in its core of seeds,
coming moments, more life (just as a tale
necessarily leads to others; the mortal

becomes mythical; the author's life
becomes the hero's; the hero's, the reader's;
so the mythical turns mortal again;
and memory sings an endless rondeau
to the beat of wings and fruitfall;
and the sun drops, too, as the clouds turn
the color of bruises; and between sunlight
and moonlight, the garden's blossoms glow,
the shadows deepen, and the statues there
uphold pale, limbless torsos, white faces
chipped and scarred—less like gods, more like clowns;
and from bough to bough, the birds perch and join,
randomly, off-key, memory's rondeau;
and the garden, freed from the tyranny
of perfection, flutters its foliage,
leaves turn to paper, and a hill arches
its back, and the branches there begin
flapping, fanning the air in breezy
transformations: the garden becomes
an angel who hovers between two worlds,
mortal and mythical—a guardian
with pages for wings, a guardian whose soul
is made by the stains of words, and who loves
both worlds, and never loves only one
to hurt the other, but honors both. . .).
Blossom to fruit to seed to tree to blossom
to fruit, and so on, a poem is never done,
though it may pass away to memory;
but protean even there, it disseminates
through an efflorescence of wings and words;
in this moment of recall the poem
is both maddeningly material and
immaterial, words on the tongue, but
not words on the tongue because
merely the memory of them, their sense.
In his more pompous interjections,
he argued that this ambiguous state

was as simple as modern physics,
and he relished in pointing out that
the universe is mostly empty space,
and that poems appropriate forgetfulness
in the same way that matter and energy
are organized around and within nothing,
the emptiness the yellowing lace needs
for its design, the pauses in memory's
rondeau, the spaces fallen angels need
for their fruitful detachment, the moments
(between moments) between moments . . .

60.

With his broken sword, the angel stoked the campfire.
In our oasis, smokestacks grew between palm trees;
so we rested and reviewed our madly various saga
in the shade of fronds and sour clouds. Our caravan
had dispersed into many, unable to compose a single
tribal tale. The desert was parcelled into storytelling
and nonstorytelling zones, as each caravan claimed its own
Word and Author. Meanwhile, godless, we found it easy to bear
the emptiness; it was one more space in which to pour
the new, alluring costumes. Sometimes we found the zealots
amusing, as they always seemed to write and speak in
uppercase letters. As our camels snored, we resumed our tale.
Our jobless hero was meeting with the Head Headhunter of
Executive Career Horizons. When she asked what position
he preferred, he raised his eyebrows provocatively. When
she asked again, he said he'd like an empty office in which,
alone, he'd read the metaphysical poets. He thanked her
when she said to return when he was ready to work. He went home
and wrote a long, windy epistle to his wife, who complained
that he sometimes used too many words to discuss words—
that it was all so many maddening mirrors. He shrugged
and with the swipe of a wing cleared the dust

from the page; and there with long histories of human
use, confusion, assertions of power—entering
new domains and losing others—they stood,
not one, but many: the words.

61.

Dear X, Another extravaganza will surely begin
without us. The gods and goddesses moisten
their lips. Long, flickering curves,
like the quivering air above deserts,
mirages on hot sand—they rise where
the tribes pitch their scrappy tents
to rest within their homes' cool,
stale air. Freud said we are dedicated to
what we were; Hollywood says we are
dedicated to the gorgeous future,
the one we will never hold. There,
between the dark couches and all
the flashy sets, the undulations
of angels stir the atmosphere, their wings
fanning the dark and sun-struck faces,
to resuscitate the diminished breath
of the present.

62.

Someone once told our fallen hero that
his wife possessed "a fine, hourglass figure."
A halo, a wedding ring, a crater,
and a crown are circular, and circles
symbolize eternity, an ending
that always returns to a beginning.
It's odd to wear eternity on your
head or finger since we usually expect
eternity to fly beyond this world
into others, but as Archimedes

and other mathematicians would show
eternity if *here*, deepening this world
with endless interludes; and the Internal Eternal
may be more practical, less demeaning
than aspiring to the insanely high,
sapphire courts and condominiums of heaven.
Love's nature is endlessly self-seeking
like all irrational or transcendental
numbers, of which *pi* is the most famous.
Love feels most—but never quite entirely—
whole when waging a kiss between the past
kisses of memory and the future kisses
of the imagination; of course, no single sequence
of kisses is love's exact equivalent;
similarly, the ratio of a circle's
circumference to its diameter is
pi (3.14159 . . .), a number whose digits stretch,
with pleasure, into the eternal. This,
however, does not mean we can forego
time's relentless sacrifice and become
immortal. To say you sacrifice sacrifice
means you do not count yourself among
the living—a useless representative
of eternity, a nameless crater, a suicide,
an equation that cancels itself and equals
zero, the still blank sand, a still hourglass.
Measuring our slow fall within time,
even without exact equivalents,
we can draw circles, tell what happened,
and make love. In the park's yellowing leaves,
he wanted simply to walk, with his arm
around his wife's waist.

63.

He woke, feeling embarrassed by his own
nakedness. He still had dreams of drowning himself,
although now he always had second thoughts, and

he began gasping, swimming, and groping for
the rocks of the shore; and a few times,
his hand would find a hold, and it was
the breast of a marble statue, an ex-lover,
or his distant wife. Circular wave within wave
within wave, and so on—that's one aspect
of the eternal, although it's often personal
like a wedding ring, or thoughts you may have
while in the shower. Farming in strange ways,
history irrigates the sad valleys
to grow the inward blossoms. Archimedes
discovered how to measure the true worth
of a friend's crown by formulating
what weight of gold displaces what volume
of water; this came to him while soaking
in the tub; and distracted by his thoughts,
he leapt from the water and ran through town,
still naked, to tell his friend the news.

64.

Once, the womb swaddled him in darkness, in flesh;
he had no illusion then of owning
the darkness, or flesh; as unassuming,
birds are intermediary spirits,
perched on fences between one property
and the next, or circling, as numbers do,
between the imaginary and the real.
The king laughed at his friend's nude arrival
and heard the formula, for which he was
grateful. From his royal wardrobe, he gave
the mathematician a purple robe. Naked, then
overdressed like a messenger who thinks himself
greater than his message, Archimedes
went walking along the citadel's walls.
He watched the birds turning, rising over
the city's heat, then dipping to the sea.

He saw couples preen, laugh, and flirt as they left
the gymnasium. Another crowning achievement—
Eros incorporates ownership's pride: a statuesque
body slips from stylish material to consume
a well-kept body posing amid elegant belongings.
He saw the sun depart and repossess
its gilding; and he saw the god of wine,
the goddess of love—their statues—tarnish.
He undressed and draped the robe over
the god's head. He wore the darkness home.

65.

Dear X, The old man died in his sleep with few regrets,
except our own. Guilt is the muddy, undrinkable river,
but we must sit beside it and see how the water nudges,
then surrenders to the banks or red clay.
The twice-fallen may decide to spare themselves,
lifting the soiled bedsheets of remorse
over their heads—ghosts playing ghosts,
just as the city, at night, throws a pale shroud
of light over its head, obscuring the starlight.
Water seeks its own level and surely this says
something about the middle class. In our lower backs,
we have useless muscles, vestigial remnants of
the body's early design, when we had tails; likewise,
guilt still twitches in our chests although the
moral frame of things collapsed ages ago.
In elementary school, there was a boy named Charles,
who had been born with a deformed rib cage, splayed
too far apart to protect vulnerable organs;
but the doctors wired the bones together; and so,
defying nature, Charles went to school and, I recall,
became a precocious lecher. I'm fond of my memory
of Charles because he was held between older and
more modern laws. The latch on my grandfather's
pocketwatch has worn out from being snapped shut

so many times. The cardinal bursting into flight
saddens us because we had enjoyed its company.
When I was walking down the street, with that watch
in my breast pocket, the watch sprang open, unable
to contain itself, a tribute to the strange timing
our origins keep, although it was only an oddity,
the flutter of sadness before lunch.

66.

The moon has many craters that stare,
sockets deprived of eyes, so empty,
but filled with many ageless mysteries.
Many great prophets, poets, and lovers
were blind. Not seeing what everyone sees
is an asset, since there in the dark you may bump,
chest to chest, into a twice-fallen angel who
takes your apology, then your hand, leading you
to a Soho loft where every wall upholds
a mural of truth; and breathless, you take in
the artist and the art at the same time;
but the end of all desires is not always
paradise, which is why our scientists
and poets humbly address themselves to
craters, the blasted valleys of the moon.
After long unemployment, he was hired
by a small town newspaper. He proofread
the classified ads, wrote obituaries,
some local news: school board meetings, a new
traffic light for some troublesome crossroads,
downtown's population of stray dogs.
He had made more money as a lawyer, but
he no longer defended producers of
toxic waste or self-destructing goods.
Noticing a famous death was sad, but satisfying
like learning the name of a large crater
on the moon. When his father passed away,

he filled in the familiar formula:
where he had worked, where he had lived,
who the survivors were, where and when
the services would be held. He counted
how few words it took. One lunar crater
is named after Archimedes—a bowl
of dust, a bowl of shadows and light;
but after countless cars and appliances,
carpets and furniture, knickknacks
and reproductions of old masterpieces,
minimalism is the last art for each
unfamous member of the middle class:
a few words, a name, a small stone.

67.

After drinking too much wine, we decided
the laws of the tribe were too self-effacing
and especially tough on the womenfolk, but since
we were so busy with foreign wars, the harvest,
and turning Archimedes' screw, the quest for self
was something we could only do on holidays,
and between holidays—fighting, irrigating,
planting, and building—you usually forgot
where you had left off; so narcissism did not
become a major problem until we had massive
amounts of leisure time, when we began watching
the moon's reflection in the ocean and saw that
water symbolized our unconscious depths,
which made poets plumbers of the sublime.
Archimedes, by the way, invented his screw
in the third century, B.C. It's a long
spiral tube on a central shaft, which one
can rotate and thereby lift low-lying water
to a higher plane. Once we became creatures
of pleasure, we realized this device
was a fine emblem for good dialogue, poetry,

sex, or anything involving our unconscious;
and this pleased Archimedes although, before,
he had been a very practical man.

68.

Ripeness is all, but only when there's a
preponderate level of fruitfulness. The new
irrigation raised that level; and since we had
already eaten the forbidden fruit, since we had
already fallen, we went back to the garden
and gorged ourselves. The wilderness became orchards
and real estate; and the undulating coils of a dream,
half-serpent, half-machine, began to spiral through
our sleep; and we grew so oddly detached —
the overripe apples the wind had shaken loose.

69.

A playground is a twice-fallen paradise —
not God's original gift, but a space
we clear for our children. The supermarkets'
winter tomatoes, too, are twice-fallen —
like tomatoes, but really the product
of a corporate conglomerate's fruitful dream —
bred thick-skinned with tough pulp so they can be
boxed, shipped, and piled without costly breakage.
His father had grown tomatoes, tender,
sweet, unctuous, and true; and he himself
was his father's fruit. Watching your children's
children is, of course, a more cherished form
of twice-fallenness; but he had refused
to make his father a grandfather; so
their family branch was bare, and no work
of art or commerce could rectify that.
His father had outlived his wife, his friends,

and his family, except his only son,
whose heart heaved in his chest, like fruit broken
against the ribs of a fallen crate. He watched
six strangers carry his father, his box
to the grave.

70.

As he set his alarm before bed, snow
fell, and he hoped for a really deep snow
that enjoyed being itself, that would fall,
enshroud the city, leaving business-as-usual
snuffed, and children playing in its wake.
To supplement his small wages as a
rookie reporter, he did part-time, para-
legal work. The secretary with whom
he shared an office was in the habit
of smoking and talking through the left side
of her mouth; and she was prone to salting
all her talk with the expletive
like. She'd say, "It was, like, amazing, like
the best winter vacation ever." Nothing fell
true to itself, only somewhat close. He woke
to the swishing of cars outside, and heard
the snow turning to rain; and by his own
backwash of wishes, off-center himself,
he followed her meaning, but had trouble
explaining why he had chosen to be,
instead of a lawyer, like a lawyer—
so he could, more truly, represent himself?
In the querulous rain, he walked to work,
treading his reflection again. Like a son, but
without father and mother, like his own man,
but still his wife's, like a lawyer, but
judged himself. . . In the scales of desire,
everything is measured against itself,
and found sadly lacking; so he was sentenced

to pay his regrets, with the provision
that he do so through good works, which, he found
required time, which required money, which led
to familiar streets of exhaust and rain.
Half-satirical, half-sympathetic,
the sky continued to empty its purse
of weather—a muddle of tenderness
and legal tender. Like a refusal of love
after a long, engaging glance, or like
some shadowy scrim that closes between
scenes of boyhood and manhood—the snow
had turned to rain, and he knew
the pure promise was lost.

71.

Dear X, When I lived in The Visionary City,
I spun great tales about my adventures in
The City of Practical Delights, which seemed
to belittle everything The Visionary City
represented; *that* was the problem with
The Visionary City: it was always representing
something beyond itself; it never simply was
itself. Now I've retired to The City of
Practical Delights; I find there, too,
you can't fulfill desire; you can only
displace it, as a ship displaces water;
and, of course, it's desire that keeps identity
afloat. I have known evenings of this
buoyancy, rowing for you, and you
for me, reaching harbor and home; and I
persist for the chance that those moments
will continue. It's ludicrous how we
try to invent our own pantheon: how
this figure stands for innocence,
this figure for loss, this one for lust,
that one, our just reward, and so on.
Occasionally, a figure will stride

into your quarters, whose gorgeous attributes
include the virtues of both major and minor
deities; and you know you will soon fall
in love, or to deep regret. I know, too,
sometimes I forced the moment to its
crisis, just so I would have a story to tell.
We would like to believe that we gently
surrendered our youth, friends, and lovers
to their own paths; but really, we were forcing
them to become our fables; so of course,
they left us to sail less navigated seas.
Please return. I'm sorry. And I am yours.

72.

Although they pass around us and within us,
the circles of eternity never require
us for their center, although geometry
served Archimedes well when he designed
some rather sophisticated catapults.
Living in a harbortown as he did,
Archimedes saw many fine sunsets,
red and gold clouds on the red and gold sea,
but never a horizon as brilliantly redundant
as when the Roman navy invaded: he saw
the sun's fire through fire. The catapults
shuddered and sang, launching balls of fire
to arch through the air and then dash themselves
upon the decks and sails of Roman ships;
he heard the cries beneath the blazing sheets,
the infernal clouds; and then went home
to take a bath and sulk, to formulate,
in simple algebra, how a heavy crown
displaces the self. When the city fell,
finally, the Roman soldiers found him
drawing circles within circles, as he
pinpointed and relinquished
his immaterial center.

73.

The ancients say that in marriage a man is king
in the same way that God is Lord over us all; but
twice-fallen and postmodern, they preferred a more
poetic reading of common law: a husband's desires
are allegories for his wife's, and vice versa; so each,
in turn, represents the other; and when they fail
to do so, their verse is only vice, and then they must
collaborate in holy and reflective revision.
In love's puzzling circle, between any two faithful
points, there are two more points, and between them,
two more, and so on—which is to say there's always room
for doubt. In the beginning was the Word, and before that,
a dark and confusing silence. Faith and Doubt are unidentical
twins and obstetricians to all profound deliveries.
The ancients say the universe is so vast because it shows
God's generosity and will; but we know it's infinite because
He's never completely sure if it's finished or not.
Why else would He create so much the same and so much
that's different, so many boring repetitions and so many
deadly surprises? For example, almost half of the
1.6 million known species here on earth are
beetles; one survey catalogued over a thousand types
in Panama alone: 683 herbivores, 296 predators,
69 fungi-eaters, and 96 scavengers. To study the richly
varied evolution of a species or vintage wine is to take
revenge against the monotony of existence. Sloppy kissing
is another way. His wife wrote and asked whether or not
he was ready to take her back and start a family.
To reply, hunched over his writing tablet, he stares
at the blankness for hours; terrified like a god
before the dawn of creation, he must say
what he means.

74.

Oh, they were an unlikely couple. When Irony first
walked into the club, we thought she was a prude

in that black dress that covered her from neck to toe.
It wasn't until she spun around, dancing with him,
we saw the kick-pleats, a flash of thigh—that the back
of her gown was scooped so unnervingly low, we could see
every muscle flicker beneath her luminous skin; it was
like watching fire within fire; and the band was entranced.
Until then, we had forgotten about Allegory—I mean,
he was only one of the regulars, a guy who always seemed
to say the obvious thing, but a generous tipper with
big hands and big feet. He was boyish, unsure, dancing
with her, but it gave his big bones some charm, some
tenderness. Closing time, the lights came up, the music
stopped; and in the lull you could hear her ask if he
would follow her home. Even the toughest guys leaned
forward and held their breath, waiting to hear
what he would say.

75.

Dear X, I would like to have children
along with a new and improved rainbow.
In the morning paper, a photograph
showed a playground in the southern suburbs
of Beirut: blindfolded, lying on the lawn there,
with his hands tied behind him, with his feet
trussed together, and with a placard hung
around his neck to announce his crime,
a Sunni Moslem was executed
by a Shiite Moslem. "More than a thousand
people looked on" as the rifle chattered
and bullets punctuated the placard,
the man, the sentence of law. A rainbow
first appeared after rain fell for forty days
and forty nights; it was God's signature
on a covenant of mercy, his promise
that never again will He destroy the world
with water—the least of our worries now
since, a crater here, a crater there, we have

many means of accomplishing The End,
and in less time than it would take to read
one page of the Bible, the Koran, or any
plaintiff's suit. There's no covenant of mercy
until we write one ourselves; meanwhile, where
do the children play?

76.

She sent postcards from Paris, pictures
of cathedrals with fragmented sentences
on the reverse sides, and he recalled
his adolescent, hormonal brainstorms,
when he wrote long, glorious epistles
in love's name, and how not even the most
elastic sentence, stretching with pleasure,
could keep love intact. With their mail taking
as long as two weeks, their correspondence
was out-of-sync, as if he were watching
a foreign movie badly subtitled in English;
so he understood the actress's lines long after
her lips had stopped moving; but even badly
represented, their trials were awarding
each of them to the other; and he anticipated
the final scene, when the screen flashes,
they kiss, and for the moment, there is no need
for interpretations.

77.

What's marvelous about Archimedes' screw
is how it allows water to be unlike itself,
to flow upstream. In the twice-fallen
scheme of things, your guardian angels should
always pose the inverse to your ratios
of id and ego, self and other; so

if you're the straight man, an angel becomes
the funny man; if you wax into a hefty
moon, an angel wanes, razor-thin—so that,
should the need arise, you're prepared to be
unlike yourself, to rise to the occasion.
He exercised regularly and ate less.
He uncorked the port of forgetfulness,
but no longer poured himself the hard liquor
of oblivion. He enjoyed the wines
of communion again, even when they were slightly
imbalanced. When he broke bread, he remembered
his wife. In short, he drank and was happy
with less. Meanwhile, his angels gorged themselves
on a buffet of various mysteries—the sandpipers,
for example, who fly from the tropics and land,
each spring, on the beaches by his hometown.
Clawing and pecking by sand, eating the eggs
of horseshoe crabs until they can barely stagger,
the birds enjoy a gluttonous, week-long layover
before flying as far as 2,000 miles, non-stop,
to the arctic, where they settle down and mate.
His wife called with her flight's estimated time
of arrival. His many selves were pecking at the
typewriter, scratching one text, then another,
plucking and feeding on many seaside
meditations—on love and truth and all
the awesome distances between. Ravenous,
they prepared for the long flight.

78.

Dear X, For the airiness, the delicacy of their bread,
for the spaciousness, the elegance of their cathedrals,
one must admire the French. The high, arching vaults
they built so thinly, letting the buttresses answer
the walls at critical points; these points enthrall
the modern soul: where desires become our sustaining

graces, like air, brick, our daily bread;
and where necessities appear as lighter
elements of our choosing, and not the animal
limits that hoop us in, ribs within flesh, maintaining
the redundant heart. Every moment of solitude
gives itself to you as would a cathedral: you withstand
yourself alone, completing the separate labors
your company holds you for. And every moment, too,
bears a little martyr—a thin gold chain
with its minute cross resting upon
a lover's chest. Where dream crosses fact,
vulnerable and impervious as skin, we see
our farfetched ideals and feel what we're allowed;
and the dream suffers at the casual brutality
of things as they merely are; so there is always
a little pity in a kiss, for our lofty dreams
are deposed, but so closely we hold them still.
For business or pleasure, we travel; and
indulging ourselves in a world that needs us,
we draw the contrails of our evening flights,
the pale, tenuous lines of our blueprints.
We work. We break bread. We hold our own.

79.

He heard many writers lament that they
were masters of a haunted house since words
are only the ghosts of what they signify,
unable to become the things themselves.
He felt, however, that these writers whined
like overly affluent consumers
who wanted more than their fair share, although,
it's true, language does frustrate one's desire
for a starry atonement of two spirits
since, always ghostly, even on their knees,
words are at best the ghosts of those two souls.
Reflectively luminous, like the moon, these ghosts

mouth, only a muzzle of flesh and bone.
Subject to falling stars, strange erasures,
he wants to do more than just wipe away
the caustic trail of tears.

82.

Across the empty expanse, love and loneliness
had drawn them back together, and he worried
they were cranking up the cantankerous machinery
of planets and gravity, predictable seasons.
A misguided creator, he had once made
a dimly redundant solar system
in which he had revolved around himself;
(and hollow be thy father's name when he will be
as he always has been, the same, the same . . .)
but from his own strange creation, he had
fallen—a happily uncentral man who vowed
to circle other lights, to collaborate only
on works forever unfinished, for there's
no keeping true love, only its making.
Before leaving the party, she took his
hand and pressed it to her chest, and he felt
warmed up to his luminous and proper orbit.
In the old days, he would hear angels laugh
over their cocktails; and he would hate them
for laughing at him, his sad, wayward fall;
but now he sees the merry-go-round spin and heave
and the clamor of angels as they climb on and off;
and now, part of their circle, he offers them
a friendly nod, and half a smile.

83.

Open to the thrashing air, delirious rain and starlight—
making love without birth control is like roaring off
in a convertible with the roof down, rushing beneath

a dubious sky, swerving along a three lane highway where
past, present, and future stretch for breathless miles, curving
over vernal valleys and mountains. Thrilled and somber,
they knew they were leaving themselves behind, that they
were hurtling towards becoming a mysterious threesome.
Though godless, he says a little prayer, that their love
was, is, and always will be far from done, in the name of
the father, the mother, and their growing love. Amen.

84.

Many claim to know, without a doubt, the identity
of the eccentric Potter who shaped the universal spheres;
smug in their knowledge, they do, on the Potter's behalf,
violence. Books burn, shops explode, and the sphere turns
its scars to the light. Marred and slightly asymmetrical,
this world is rounded with a little sleep, but the Potter
had shaped it first. With one foot fidgeting in doubt,
and with the other pedaling the wheel of faith,
the Potter held the clay between the opposing hands
of love and humility—in a grasp like that
of prayer, all the while turning it, and molding
an imperfect but holy sphere, one of many;
but just how many and why is anyone's guess.
Archimedes calculated how many grains of sand
it would take to fill the universe. He arrived
at the wrong sum; but with all the sad emptiness,
the gaping fears, the vast ennui, it was inevitable,
like our confusing suns with gods and gods with
potters. Unable to count the number of angels
on the head of a pin, we asked an angel to estimate;
he only said that the filigree of wings, the undulation
of bodies, stretched baroquely from horizon to horizon.
In twice-fallen cosmology, the self is a sphere
containing a vast number of spheres and an even vaster

emptiness. The number of possible flings on any sphere
clamors towards the infinite; and without our star charts,
the longitudes and latitudes of love, we would surely
lose our bearings.

85.

"Love makes love," his mother would often say;
"And money makes money," his father would add;
and now that they were gone, he wondered
what they had meant by their aphoristic
duet. Srinivasa Ramanujan, a modern
mathematician, has left a legacy
of dog-eared notebooks, in which many brave
formulae march on parade, but without proof
of their heroism. Ramanujan worked mostly
with chalk on slate; so his sleeve erased
the records of their early countdowns and liftoffs,
including how he came to launch such a
ponderous, new equivalent for a ratio
of *pi*. His notes are like the odd sayings
that each generation leaves for the next—
old flyers who fail to recall their first
test flights through the burn of impassioned orbits
and the chilling vacuity of space.
Only after a computer chattered
and calculated the value of *pi*
to 17 million places—only then could they prove
why Ramanujan's insight was correct. Fables,
epistles, the soft numbers of verse—writing
for his wife and their as yet unconceived children,
our unnamed, undecorated hero was figuring
a problem to its umptieth digit
to recover an original proof,
procreative and true.

86.

One goes to galleries to see a favorite
painting and to be seen by others as you
stand before it, as if you were saying
to the jury, "See the evidence: this
is my sorrow; this, my virtue; see how deeply
I cherish them." She loved the Dutch because
they had built their homes below sea level,
a real-life allegory of souls beneath desire;
so they went to see the works of old masters,
but the museums were mobbed, an impure market—
everyone taking her soulful emblems for their own,
or making dumb remarks about the style, her virtues.
She grew sullen and sad, but that night they made love
meticulously, as they themselves were the only
testimony they could swear upon.

87.

The serenity of paintings is a consolation;
take Vermeer's "Young Woman with a Water Jug"
for instance—its fabulous morning light.
Even the shadows have the faint luminescence
of pearls. Vermeer admired how each thing
apprehends, then surrenders the light,
so that the water jug is minutely lit
by the sun and everything in the room, their colors,
the woman's blue dress, the alabaster walls,
the rich, oriental brocade on the table—
all send the light back upon itself,
as if in a judicious sentence of mercy,
whereby the light is free, but must take on
a quality of everything it strikes
in its casual embraces. Although she
is wearing a wimple, the woman is no
ecstatic nun, ready for the raiments

of heaven, for celestial light. No,
she is glad to be holding, with one hand,
a finely crafted jug, and to be opening,
with her other hand, the casement window.
She is about to water a flowerbox of tulips.
Outside, the ships sail away from the wharves
only as fast as the wind will take them. This
is seventeenth century Holland, before
advertising would show everyone driving,
dancing, or flying out of the frame to buy
an alluring style, a life greater than
what capitalism itself can provide.
The painting, however, is political
only insofar as it flatters the homes
of middle class merchants, their love of maps
and fine imports; but those details of the painting
are nothing compared to the gratitude
of light, its material and immaterial
radiance. Vermeer, surely, painted that light
in a moment of innocence, remembering when
he kissed a girl before the levees. Only a boy,
he didn't desire, or know how, to go beyond
a kiss; so the light in the painting redounds
lightly upon itself. Secular and still holy,
the jug is filled with water and all
the colors of the room.

88.

Sometimes it is necessary to be rude to people
in order to maintain the pumps and levees because,
always, you are losing your land to the sea's
relentless appropriation; and you do not want
to join the formlessness of eternity too soon.
Please everyone and you are no one, the face
into which your lunch date yawns at noon.
It's another thing, however, to seem servile

and keep an aloof, manipulative center;
and sometimes this is fun, like crucifying
hundreds of masks to the branches of a tree.
I'm surprised at how often Christian imagery
surfaces like a breathless dolphin in my
ratiocinations. Perhaps, it's because Christianity
was the first alphabet I learned for spelling
my dreams; and so I see all succeeding ruminations
through those holy letters. Although an atheist,
I don't resent this condition too much since
it prevented me, as a child, from coveting
the chrome wings on the crass angels of commerce,
the long fins of old Cadillacs, for example.
And maybe, too, language can only embrace
the static, and the static is not serene,
not love, love; so we expel words,
but what we dive for, too playful, too fluid,
is beyond them; and like dolphins, dear, we swim
in one element, but must breathe another.

89.

It's the end of a quarter, not a phase
of the moon, but of the passing tax year.
The stockholders' reports are dispatched
with due solemnity, but Being is only the
pregnant pause before Non-being's punchline.
During lunar eclipses, Aztec mother put
obsidian in their mouths to ward off
evil, to protect their unborn; and this
resembles our uses of language, the dark ink
of a poem, petition, or bedtime story.
Desire is endless, but we are not.
I am not you; that's my grief; but you
are not I; that's your virtue. An obvious
symptom of twice-fallenness is
telling time by clocks and calendars

instead of the heavenly cycle of stars.
I have failed to balance my books, for the moon
has meddled with the rising and falling sums;
but despite the tentative muddle, the cloudlike
smudges, the obscured net worth, I know
laughter will be the bottom line.

90.

Since the self is a sphere, it may stare inwards
across its own diameter and see its deepest inclinations
on the opposing side. What one may feel within this
distance from one's self is alienation, but within this
womb-like gulf, one may also hold an aesthetic, comic, or
scientific distance, a prerequisite for love's artful labors.
He scanned the expanse, the hard shadows and light, and saw
his unruly feet, his own footprints in the sand. He sees
the archangel with his broken sword, inscribing the sand
with circles and blank verse; and he knows his story
has come full circle, with its odd, iambic
parameters.

91.

We decided to spend the afternoon
in a state park between two cities.
Gabriel had to whisper in Mary's ear
to explain the news, since the miracle
had settled upon her as gently as light
or pollen on a windowsill. The divine
conception blossomed in the time it takes
God to cultivate a thought, which is
no time, since God introduced all thoughts
to Himself long ago. If all ideas
became deed so directly, rhetoric
would become obsolete; and the stratagems
of love and eroticism, the masks of art,

the exuberant shades of poetry—all
would perish. A terrible, lonely thing—
to be God, when all the lights fantastic
remain only a prismatic show of light
whose colorful components you know
all too well, because they're all your own.
Lugging a worn blanket and picnic basket,
we follow the park's circular path.
I admire your limbs and the shadows cast
through your sheer, summer dress. Godless,
we are blessed with our ungodliness.
In your ear, I whisper a ludicrous
proposition, and still walking within
the moment's limits, you can only laugh.

Photo by Carol Campbell

D. W. Fenza was born in Chester, Pennsylvania in 1955. He is a graduate of the Colorado College, The Johns Hopkins University, and the University of Iowa. His poetry and critical writings have been previously published in *The Antioch Review, Poet and Critic, Open Places, Telescope,* and other literary journals. He is currently publications editor for the Associated Writing Programs in Norfolk, Virginia.

OTHER GALILEO BOOKS